M⊙RNING
LIGHT

W

W

NEW
POEMS
TOM
HARDING

PP

Morning Light

Published by Palewell Press Ltd www.palewellpress.co.uk

First Edition

ISBN 978-1-911587-78-1

A CIP catalogue record for this title is available from the British Library

Dedication

To P&E

Contents

Morning Window

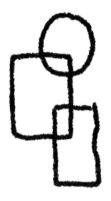

Morning Music

Listen close between the
horns and percussion
of the churning traffic

the sunlight is creaking
across the floorboards
of an attic room

the one where a fly
is buzzing in and out
as if looking for something
he left behind.

Someone is waking now
and reaching out
in an otherwise empty bed

while in the balcony below
the widow whispers
to her morning glories

and in a next door room
a caged bird is singing
with only a small mirror
for company.

Say It (Over and Over Again)

I sit by a window
and watch the street
Ornette Coleman
plays "Tomorrow Is The Question?"
But today it is spring
and perhaps it's the new dose
of Citalopram
or the double espresso
or the twelve spoons of sugar
in this Danish pastry
but everything seems possible today,
the sun is high
the sky is blue
the cars pass gleaming
and the blossom blows
like confetti
landing on the heads of
the passers-by;
the homeless man
with a tartan suitcase
and chessboard tucked
under his arm,
the woman in white
getting out of a taxi
and fixing her hair
as if late to a ceremony
that's already
in full swing.

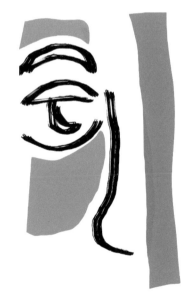

Myself When I'm Real

There is not much to separate us,
the little fly and I,
him upon the windowsill
and I upon the sofa,

two small specks
in the footnote of history,
passing time
in the thin spring light
of this pale room.

While the poplar trees
sway their shadows
on the ceiling

the fly stands still
as if in contemplation
or respect
to the mysteries of life
we will never solve.

Instead it's I who gets up
intermittently to buzz around this house;
making coffee,
picking up books
and putting them down,

peering into the fridge
I looked in minutes before,
always expectant of
a miracle
to have occurred.

I Had a Dream

I had a dream
I was serving
in a government
of the dead,

I was the bulldog
the firefighter,
the master of
the excel spreadsheet
a puller of
gold teeth

I built the pivot table
I built the filter curve
that measured every wave
that thinned out
the herd.

I dreamt I
was a lorry driver,
hauling through the night,
a forty ton
eighteen-wheeler
packed with bodies
swaying like meat
in suffocating heat.

I dreamt I was the rat
scuttling
across broken glass,
gnawing at the toes
and fingertips
of bound and gagged
bodies
in a basement
with taped windows.

I dreamt I was the fish head
rotting from
the top down

my fingers were covered
in blood and ink,

I was a skeleton in an Armani suit
with plastic ties
on my wrists
and no strings in my shoes

I was a big fat tongue
for hire
with pockets stuffed
with blood soaked
bank notes
and an offshore
account to hide
lobbied votes.

I dreamt I was the
puppet on the
parish council,
invisible hands inside
of me

I dreamt I ran for election
on an everyman
agenda,
I kept the village green
clean
and shipped
the homeless
to Rwanda.

I dreamt
I was both ends
of the equation;
I had my finger on the trigger
and my temple
on the barrel,

I was the knife
on the throat
and the hundred-foot
Russian boat.

I was the fly
crawling on the open eye
and I was the eye
too....

I was the toddler
washed up on
the beach

I was electric tape
stretched across
blood-soaked teeth

I was the skeleton
in the middle of a speech,
spewing grand gestures
and Nazi policies.

I had a dream
I was at a party
of a government of ghouls
with paper hats
on our skulls
and shopping trolleys
filled with booze

I dreamt
we were in the rose garden
pissing
in the flower beds

I dreamt we were slumped
on the podium,
thoughts and prayers
spewing out of our
heads
saying the only ones dying
were those meant
to be dead.

I dreamt we were ghosts
I dreamt we were mist
I dreamt we were
the fountain pen
and the fist.

It's Easy to Remember

A fly motoring through
the open window
disturbing the soft slumber
of the
summer morning.

Two on the street chatting;
one jangling keys
the other tugging
a dog sniffing a lamppost.

A delivery man
in shorts,
unloads parcels
from a
brown truck, whistling
as he goes.

A woman in blue
now a car passing,
now a dog barking

now sparrows
leaping into
the green trees,
singing the world
alive.

The Biology of Loss

We're always
forgetting
little things;
like death
or our own
belief in nothingness,
neither of which
are any use
when you're
going about
in the world trying
to enjoy
yourself.

This morning
the wind blows
the green leaves
while we eat
Turkish Eggs
with yogurt and
black coffee,

we are
grieving nothing,
at least in any way
we might
recognise.

Master of Nothing

My dream is
a calendar
white as snow,
days spent
drinking coffee
with nowhere to go,
doodling
in the margins
of the Sunday papers.
A barefoot bystander
to the latest disaster,
standing in the kitchen,
chewing a yellow pencil,
staring out the window
when the wind
blows the trees
and the sparrows
chirp alarm in the leaves
and the cat passes below
thinking
he's unseen.

Spring Cleaning

Early morning
fresh breeze
coming down
the hillside
the cedar trees
holding the sun
in their leaves,
the sea
glimmering
brightly,
the beach
quiet except
for the clacking
of pebbles, the tide
lifting to sweep
beneath them
before softly
setting
them back down.

Morning Coffee

The Process

This morning the inner critic
is playing all the hits;
how I should have jumped
out of bed at dawn
to do star jumps,
sumo squats,
push ups

followed by
a cold shower
and ten minutes
of deep breathing,
then an immunity boosting
breakfast of
boiled water with lemon,
rolled oats blended with
flaxseed, broccoli
and coconut water.

Twenty minutes
of morning pages,
sun salutations
and gratitude practice,
where I repeat
mantras of
love and kindness
for all living things,

even the neighbour
returning from his
morning jog,
doing lunges
outside my kitchen
window,
forever a step ahead
on the eightfold path
to better health

or is it the ten pillars
to a happier self?

I can't remember
as pour my
black coffee
and lift the remains
of a vanilla creme
almond glazed
donut
to my lips,

which I halved
with wisdom and restraint
yesterday morning.

Napkin Equation

Finishing a cortado
on a wet morning in October,
I wonder how much coffee
I've drunk in my life.

I do a quick calculation
based upon twenty years of coffee drinking
where, roughly, three cups a day,
if a typical cup
is two hundred and twenty-five millilitres of liquid,
comes to four million nine hundred
and twenty-seven thousand
and five hundred millilitres of coffee
or
one thousand and eighty-three point
three imperial gallons,

which is enough to fill forty bathtubs
or an eight foot by six-foot plunge pool
(according to poolandspa.com)
but which still does not seem
as much coffee as I imagined,
picturing instead at least an average size
swimming pool,
or even a good way onto
an Olympic size pool,
which I've been slowly topping up
through the course of my life.

An Olympian task I will complete
with a last espresso drunk on my deathbed,
whereupon I will close my eyes
to envision this deep reservoir,
vast as an ocean and stretching
in all directions,

the distant shore of my past
behind me,
and the vast darkness
of the unknown ahead,
infinite and black,
tempered only by a dash of milk.

I'm Old Fashioned

I try being present,
but my mind
takes me where I don't want to be,
travelling
back and forth in time
so I anchor
myself with coffee,
watching
the steam rising
in the golden
mid-morning sun,
and
mutter prayers
of love and kindness
to every bowed face
passing the window
in blustery spring winds,
blissfully unaware
of their role
in the morning ritual.

Small Mercies

The route to happiness
is to expect less of things,
so they say,

leave alone the sorrow,
the slaughter and
put your feet up awhile

marvel at the
small mercies materialising
before you;

the universe of dust
in the morning light,

the steam spiralling
from the coffee cup

the sparrows
leaping into the bright blue
beyond the window,

the cat breathing in his sleep

this shrinking island of time
before the world comes
lapping at your feet.

I Wish I Knew

The ones charged
with monitoring us
are elsewhere right now,

I sit with my feet up
reading about the sauropods
of the Triassic era, next
how Saturn would float
if balanced in water.

Out the window the spring breeze
ushers clouds along
and a few flustered pigeons.

I sip my coffee,
watching the steam
rise in the light of the window,

the moment cooling
in my hands.

A Few Good Things

It's good to be over forty
and to not believe
in yourself anymore,
to wake in the
early morning and lie there
meditating
on your theoretical
nonexistence.
To stand
before the mirror,
undressing the self,
realising the you
that you thought to be you
is not really a you at all.

To go about your day,
conceptualising yourself
as a sort of machine,
systematically
ticking off obligations:
buying envelopes,
paracetamol and
oranges.

It's good to drink coffee,
and walk along
in the breeze
like a cloud drifting along
towards the heart of the city
that springs to greet you

responding only
to the dumb animal
of your inner being
that's overcome
with longing, for what,
you don't quite know.

Guest House

Sipping coffee
in an empty room,
sand on the wooden floor,
light reflected
in a driftwood mirror,
shadows moving across
the white-washed wall.

The sea still and bright,
a boat with
its white sail,
moving or staying still
you can't quite tell.

Morning Breaths

October Poem

Do not be scared
you are beautiful
the leaves are falling,
we are huddled together
and the wind is blowing,
the lime trees sway
the sails of a ship turning
their outstretched arms
scrape along the roof
and tap at the glass,
we're shivering
in corners where
spiders are blindly
weaving.

Some days you wake up
and cannot recall
who's dead and who's living,
you flick through your memory
like an old notebook
and find nearly every page filled.

It is autumn
and the leaves are falling,
your mother is a fallen leaf,
your dog is a fallen leaf,
wave to them,
they're looking back at you,
offering you
a place to fall.

In A Lonely Place

You were the gumshoe
with a drinking problem,
always too gullible
for your own good,
always in the shadow of some danger,
always risking your life,
ever at the mercy of being ambushed
down a blind alley,
on the errand of
some mysterious blonde.

No wonder you
ended up here;
watching the rain-soaked street
with your feet up
nursing an ice pack on
your brow.

No wonder you can't remember
your own name,

No surprise,
whenever you
open a new case,
the man in the photos
looks just like you.

Days of Wine and Roses

A morning
as good as any,
you step outside and breathe
amongst the moving trees
and say Geez!
I'm alive,
Imagine that!

You and the cat,
padding barefoot
across the courtyard's warm
dusty concrete.

Admiring the
green leaves
and poppies poking
out the cracked
concrete,

the neighbour's great
sunflower nodding
his head
as if to say,
how do you do?

While the cat rolls
at your feet,
on a day so sweet
it will not
go down in history.

Hungry Ghost Poem

Beautiful to wake
on the first Monday
in January
and realise
you don't exist,
at least
in any way
you might imagine.

The watery light
filling the room,
the particles
of your constructed self
dissolving in the breeze
of the open window

like the seeds
of the dandelion
in the spring wind,
leaving a heavy head
nodding on
its hollow stem.

Original Face

You have no control
and yet you suffer for it.

Out of the darkness
thoughts rise
from a dark pond
fed by a turbulent stream,

they break the surface,
multiplying, a frenzy
of carp mouthing
for the crumbs
of your attention,

until all is still again;
a dark mirror
reflecting the night sky,
the stars,
the moon
white and empty
as your
original face.

Moment's Notice

Lying here under
the grim weight
of my own expectations,
believing my life
should be
somehow different or other
to what it is,

I focus on my breath
falling in and out
and become aware of
my neck and chest,
taut like
the chains of a clock
geared in anticipation
to the moment
arriving next.

I focus on my belly,
rising and falling,
as the cat enters
and jumps to the bed
to look at me.

Relax, he says,
nothing is required today,
except lying here
embracing your
total unimportance
to the world.

While out the window
the trees nod,
and the sparrows hop,
and a distant plane
passes west,
leaving a vapour trail
which soon
dissolves
to nothing.

Breaking News

A single tear,
landing on the morning newspaper
causes you to
shuffle the pages
clear your throat
and read the next headline,
another report
from the farthest corners
of the unexamined self
that primitive place
where the mothers
are all hysterical
and tragedy waits
on every corner.

Noumena

It's lonely,
all morning
I chase the shadows
on the cave wall.

I raise my hand
and lower it
thinking myself
into action, always
a few milliseconds
behind the eight ball.
I scratch my beard
I drink coffee,
who owns this shipwreck?
I hear the captain say.

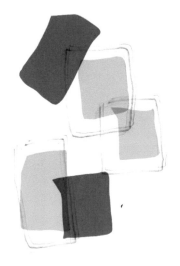

The windows
are all broken,
I am a bystander
talking myself into existence;

the ghosts of the culture
blowing through
my thoughts.

Birds fly
up and down,
the octopus
changes colour
in his sleep
while dreaming
in black and white.
You're adrift,
the captain says,
it is only January

and the waters are
dark and choppy
ahead.

Morning Heartache

Where Are You?

You make me feel warm
enough to be alive
I want to say but don't.

Time is short
at least that's how it feels,
as though we only have
this moment
before it's lost.

We're the last
of the resistance
in the back room of
a Parisian café,

we're strangers
stranded
in an airport bar
as the snow swirls outside.

Meet me here
a year from now,
I want to say
as you get up from
the table and walk away
without a glance.

Has Anyone Ever Told You?

You look like a goddess
in the dawn
or perhaps a saint
in stained glass,
nothing beneath your
skin but light.

You are
an oil painting,
two bathers beneath the moon
or a golden parrot
perched in a mango tree,
or the woman
bent down cradling
a bowl of fruit.

You look like
the last statue standing
in a bombed out
town square,

a porcelain Aphrodite
shrouded in smoke
and dust,

the last hopes
of humanity
resting in your
silent face.

First Date

Sometimes
I feel alone,
trapped inside the bony dark
of my skull,
when the wind blows
and the trees scrape the roof
it feels like my heart might burst.

Sometimes I think
the only material capital
in the universe
is loneliness
and the shared
longing for love.

Do you believe in
life after death?
Do you believe in God?

Sometimes
I feel like a flying ant
nestled inside
the bright head
of a daisy,
the universe
a blurry mystery
above my head.

When my mother died
I couldn't stop crying
at inappropriate times
I left a meeting mid-sentence
and sat in a toilet
cubicle
with my head in my hands.

Am I oversharing?

Sometimes
I think I would like to be a dog,
snoozing and untroubled
by nothing
beyond the mystery
of my own desires,
sniffing the occasional
wet street,
or lying listening
to the breeze,
contemplating the big
questions;
like what happens
inside a black hole
or how do you know
if you've ever been in love?

Have you been in love?
Sometimes
I think I'm only
in love with my phone.

When I was a teenager
I used to recite the names
of everybody I loved
every night before I slept
otherwise they might
drop dead.
I believed the contents
of my mind
and the world
were the same.

Sometimes I feel,
like I am vanishing,
like am a nameless man
in a photo kept
in a shoebox
beneath a floorboard
of a vacant house.

Sometimes I feel
like a ghost
or an extra
in a silent film.

Do you have a favourite film?

Sometimes
I feel
like a dog
trapped
in a capsule

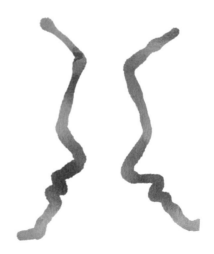

in the cold
darkness of space
with only small
blinking lights
for company.

Sometimes
I don't know
who I am
or what I am doing
or where I am going

Sometimes I don't believe
in anything at all
except what
is in front of me,

just as you
seem to hold together
the entire fragile framework
of all material reality
with your gaze,

but, perhaps,
I am going too fast.

Communion

It's been so long,
you have not aged
while I have become
a ghost.

We talk by
moving objects
around a
white table.

While
the breeze from the
open window
nods the heads
of the lilies,

a small
white cup
is gently lifted
then set back
down.

Maybe You'll Be There

Look at that mutt
tied up down there
on the rain-soaked street,
waiting for his special someone
to come back.

Everything is quiet,
as if the entire city has left
for the long weekend in summer,

leaving the rest to do
whatever it is ghosts do
when nobody is looking

opening and closing cupboards,
tossing a tennis ball
in darkened room.

A white face at the window
the empty street where
traffic lights flicking on and off

a dog gnawing on his lead,
who's there one minute
and gone the next.

Must I Go on Pretending

I feel redundant
like Pluto,
hanging around
on the outskirts to nowhere.
John Coltrane plays
Night Lights
I'm happily drunk
and romantically
distraught.

Mars is in the sky tonight
an orange dot,
the universe plays
the song of the spheres
spiralling around
the colossal black hole
at its heart
from which no light or matter
can escape.

The heart is a beacon
emitting small
electric pulses.

You were the one
I was calling out to
all these years,

Not that I knew
you were there,
not that I could have known
you were listening.

Spring Poem

I am not myself today
I hear myself say
But when am I myself
anyway?

I look in the mirror
I'm standing on the surface,
of what?
Somewhere within me
a sticky mass of neurons
binds together something
called memory,
which in turn forms something
like what it feels
to be me.

Time continues to shift
a trick of the light.

We drink tea
in the bright sun
of the kitchen,
the world
gleaming around us.

You and I are like the
objects on a table
in a bad still life,
floating unanchored
above the surface

no difference
to these oranges
or porcelain
Japanese coffee cups
you love so much.

At any given time
one of us
threatens to
pick up our life
and shatter it on
the floor.

What shall we do today?
You say as if calling out
from the past

I shake my head
and count my breaths,
trying to keep us alive
in the present.

December 24th

It's late; we should be driving,
But I'm losing the battle.
He is holding the toothbrush,
But now, he's smearing toothpaste
Over the fabric mouth
Of his small monkey,
Which is smiling.
So, I lie on his undersized bed,
With my oversized fatigue
Pressing into its thin springs,
Praying to no one
With all that needs to be done.
And yet, somehow later,
Miraculously, we're driving
Through near-midnight streets
Filled with dimly lit windows
Frosted with halos and small
Twinkling lights, beginning
The two-hour drive to the hospital,
Where you are waiting.
There is peace for the first time,
When he finally sleeps,
Cocooned in his woollen hat and scarf,
In the dark warmth of the car,
Heater blowing and
Radio murmuring,
Silent Night.
I glimpse him in and out
Of the sliding motorway lights,

His eyes closed, brow furrowed,
That same still seriousness
Of the baby we brought home
That second night from the hospital,
Except bigger now,
And clutching
The small, tattered monkey;
A vessel for all his belief
That he carries
Through the world,
Just as I carry him,
And he, in his way,
Carries me,
Always in love and hope,
Of finding ourselves
Safely delivered.

Morning Blues

Entropy

We have no time
for the impending heat death of the universe,
there is too much to distract
ourselves with down here.

You're quietly explaining
your heart has shifted from where it once was,
as if knocked from its orbit
by mysterious forces.

The universe tends to disorder,
your eyes say,
just like the ice melting in the glass
or the coffee cooling in the cup

or the nine-billion-year-old star
silently extinguishing
at the limits of
of observable space.

Just as dark energy
pushes stars from their planets
and your eyes detach
from mine
and your fingers
let go of my hand.

Every Time We Say Goodbye

The light of a family dinner flickers
in the glass eye of the universe,

a film where nobody is talking, rather everybody is talking but
nobody is listening

a table of animated faces, sat in their favourite places,
warmed in the golden light of the early cosmos.

A billion-dollar telescope floats through the silent vacuum of space,
It opens its golden wings to peer into the past,

It hunts through the stars like a cat stalking through long grass.

Here your mother lies dead in her sleep, here the cat stays stuck in
his leap.

The darkness eats at the flame that enshrouds their face.

Here a baby floats through imageless space
its reality formed from abstract shapes
like the shattered pieces from a dropped plate.

A family dinner plays out in the cold darkness of space,

a table is laid but there's a missing place.

Outwards

You're getting ready
for sleep,
putting on pyjamas
like a deep-sea diver
pulling on scuba gear

or perhaps an astronaut
readying to touch down
on the cool white
surface of the pillow

but as you slip
beneath new sheets
it's obvious you're
an Arctic explorer,

stepping onto the
frozen tundra
at midnight,

the vast icy multitudes
of your unknown self
ahead of you.

Waiting for the Miracle

I hear this morning that
Leonard Cohen is dead,
which is not so surprising
as lately everyone is dying
it seems, I sit at this table
watching the steam rise
from my coffee and ask God
to reveal himself
in any way I would recognise
but he doesn't unless that's him
nodding his head amongst
the lilies in the yellow bucket
outside the florist
or perhaps he's there
forensically illuminating
the finger smears
on this plastic menu
or perhaps he is everywhere,
as they say, at any one time,
shooting back and forth
across the universe
to keep an eye on things,
like the tiny particles
bursting from the sun in their trillions,
the next moment
passing between the cavernous
space between the atoms
in my outstretched hand,
the one I'm waving now

in direction of the waitress,
who approaches
through a galaxy of dust,
ready to write down
anything I desire.

Giant Steps

The breeze
unleashes
you from your constraints,
you rise untethered
like Gulliver
stepping out
into the tide
that empties
the rush-hour Tube.
As you cross
the street,
the new world
opens before you.

Brilliant Corners

We're just beginners
compared with the
blue shark, say,
or the Komodo dragon,
only a few thousand years
under our belts.

No wonder it feels strange
to find yourself
trapped six floors up
with sealed windows
debating critical dependencies
and resource allocation
with humans you barely know.

No wonder
you wake on summer mornings
filled with an uncontrollable longing.

No wonder you don't
recognise yourself
in the passing glass of the cars
and buildings.

No wonder as you
skip across the curb
with your sleeves rolled
and teeth bared, you
grin with a hunger
that feels six billion years
in the making.

You'll Never Know

The breeze blows
above our heads,
as the ants go marching
beneath our outstretched feet,

venturing headfirst
in the winds of chance,
some doing better
some worse.

Look at this one
heading north
along your outstretched leg,
lost in confusion or calling
it's hard to tell.

The Golden Age of Poetry

Do you know the one about
the Chinese poet
whose heart was so filled
with wine and longing
he fell to his death
trying to seize the moon
beneath his small wooden boat?

Somewhere, he's still falling;
trapped in Zeno's paradox
of infinite divisibility,
where a travelling body
continually halves
the distance
between itself
and its destination
and so never arrives.

Suspended in time;
mouth open, eyes half-closed,
blissful and drunk
with delusion, happy
as any man who's lived
and died ever since.

Come On In

There's a room
upstairs
with nothing in it
except a chair
and a space to sit and watch
the sun cross the floor,
illuminating with it
a universe of dust
and warming
the floorboards
until it reaches you,
to caress your arm,
slowing moving
across your face and chest
to embrace your
body, to linger there
before
it leaves you,
sliding across
the floor and retreating
through the open door
without a word.

The Story So Far

You can put it down
at any moment,
abandon it
without regret,
do not fall for
the sunken cost
of your own
narrative,
the doctrine
of the imagined self,
no matter how far
you've come,
let it go
at any time,
discard it in
the phonebooth
on the busy street,
leave it on the
backseat
of the X7 bus,
wave goodbye
to it as it
disappears
leaving you
on the corner
of a four-way street
free to walk in every
direction.

Morning News

05.01 am

Up all night,
shuffling complaints,
I sleep, finally
consoled by
the first soft light
of morning.
No sign
of the moth
I confided with
most of the night,
flittering
at my bed light.
Gone in his
dusty overcoat,
another
refugee,
slipping out with
a suitcase
of worries
in the early dawn.

The Faithful Few

Hey God,
nothing new
down here,
just the usual
stories of survival;
the wind
ruffling the feathers
of the pigeons
pecking at the fallen
flakes of brioche
a few ants
emerging
to carry what's left,
every crumb
proof things
are still
going to plan.

Shame

How it all turned out,
with all
our gods dead
or disgraced,
dragged
from their
pedestals
and toppled
into the sea,
leaving us
here, anchored
under the
weight of our
names.

Song of John Clare

The first thing they'll tell you is that you don't exist,
they'll even prove it to you
they'll put the paperwork in front of you
saying you simply cannot be the person
you claim to be.

But, I am—yet what I am none cares or knows

Yeah that was me.
I'm John Clare you see
just as I was Byron
and Shakespeare
formerly,

I'm all of them you see
tomorrow I could be you,
maybe, I could even be me
or at least the man that
they want me to be.

It's not a mystery you see,
there's a science
to becoming someone else,
or at least unbecoming yourself.

You might say, just as a landscape
is reborn and remade
and not an atom stays the same,
a person can pass away

but his immortal soul remain.
Just like this town,
a town as old as me,
Northampton,
yeah, this town is me.

Let me tell you how it happens,
weekdays, breakfast;
poached eggs, weak tea,
a few rounds of toast
and that's me.

They let me walk into the town
and I sit on the steps
of the All Saints church
just as I've done
for two hundred years.
I write love poems for pennies,
I listen to passersby.

This morning a woman
talking about a boy,
a teenager jumped from a lorry
on the A508
turns up in a quiet village, Boughton,
knocking on doors.
he had nothing,
was asking for food,
Syrian maybe.
They gave him a can of coke
a cheese sandwich.

The police were called.
I walked the same road once,
when they imprisoned me
first time in
High Beach, Essex. 1841.
Impossible they say but
that was me.
Four days on the road
walking, sleeping
with my head pointing north.
I ate the grass on the road
the nights were filled with ghosts
feet raw,
hot days through market towns
cat called and commented
under their breath
'poor creature', they said,
'you'll be noticed'
'O he begs'

They kept me to the road,
fields gated,
The Enclosure Act in force.
A country and mind under lock and key.
Middle England,
auld England
snoozing through centuries.
A patchwork prison.
Fearful, dreaming of migrant threats.

There's a boy walking

upon the road,
he's walking through fields
endless as the sea.
Walking confirms the identity,
I've lived with mud on boots,
ever since I bounced
on my mother's knee.
Bright blue mornings,
An expanse of open fields.
I'd disappear for days at a time
towards endless horizons
not a single sign.

I'd wake drunk on my back,
middle of the day
sun on my face.
A beetle who can't get up,
a scarecrow with his mouth
sewn shut.

I am but what I am
who knows?

There's a boy upon
the road
and he walks with me
his feet are sore
his clothes are worn.

You did the right thing
they say, the gang masters
are to blame.

Nothing to be done anyway.
Where was I?
11 am. I finish my coffee and walk
I cross this town,
past vacant shops,
blackened windows
fast food,
coffee chains,
mobile phone shops.

All, lifted and dropped.
I see the woman again
buying lemons at the market square,

'What was his name?' I say.
'Who?' She said.
'The boy from Syria.'
I don't know, she said.
He's gone she said,
he ran across the fields
and did I mind not
listening in to her
conversation.

Sometimes I think about
who I was
or who I was meant to be.

That was me you see-
a boy on the road,
just another refugee.

My head's an attic of memories.
I slept under green trees,
head filled with violent
summer dreams,
a whole history of
possibilities
coming to life
inside of me.

I am—but what I am
I can no longer see.

There's a boy upon
the road
and he walks with me
and tomorrow it could be you,
well maybe,
but today I am him
and he is me.

Day Off

Funny to think of you gone
on a bright morning like this,
crossing the Euston Road
with rolled sleeves,
nothing to do;
10:12, on a Tuesday in spring.
Sky blue and dotted with clouds,
cranes swinging
in construction dust
and breeze-blown blossoms.
Workers whistling in shiny yellow hats,
the city in full swing,
as I walk away from myself
in bright cars and mirrored glass,
along streets like Paris,
except it's London in spring.
Breathing, I go with
warm lungs of idling taxis,
past sour, piss-soaked alleys,
rubbish truck fumes,
walking, walking,
with you in my head,
six months on - still dead.
Another face in the crowd,
sun slipping behind a cloud.
As I mill amongst the living
in the bright plaza of the British Library,
terra-cotta red against the blue
and the barista at the stand

in the blue dungarees
and a polka dot scarf, hands
me a heart drawn in foam.
Ah, love! I am so lost and alone.
pick up, pick up,
the dead are on the phone.
But I'm mingling with the living,
flocks of students, tourists,
the odd solitary businessman
in this amphitheatre of stone.
I watch a young man in a Picasso shirt
serenading a woman in orange,
I sit beside Newton bent
peering over his books,
I count my breaths,
learning to breathe again,
I'm beginning anew,
exorcising ghosts,
reminding myself I'm alive,
with spring in my heels,
hope in my head, I'm leaning out
for love and gratitude,
a flower bending
towards the sun;
yes, in my heart, spring has sprung!
John Coltrane plays
and the blossom falls,
April in Paris, London in Spring!
while the sun moves
in and out of clouds,
my mood goes with it.

I cross the Euston Road,
fumes and traffic, to quiet
Judd Street, past the Ethiopian supermarket,
then the Half Cup, men with flat caps,
Turkish coffee and dominoes,
the Vietnamese nail bar,
the vegan cafe, now Linda's Flowers...
what news can I send you?
The world has turned strange
and sad, or maybe that's just me.
Katherine is alone,
she misses you more than most.
Henry is moving to Scotland,
it's very sad.
We're all escaping our commitments,
like today I'm walking and walking
with nothing to do but feel
the breeze on my arm,
longing in my limbs, rudderless
a woman in a yellow dress,
two bike couriers stopped
chatting, breathing over coffee,
now a charity worker
trying to get my attention.
Hello, hello, it's me.
pick up, the skies are blue,
there's a whole world waiting
and so much to do.
what can I tell you?
I'm starting again,
feeding the white dog,

walking, naked as a notebook,
useless as the plastic bottle in my hand.
I tie my shoelace, I tighten my belt.
now a bus is stopping,
now a car is honking,
now a woman with a small
dog in her hand, quivering,
my hand... too quivering
with coffee and too much nothing,
I'm walking to where?
crossing Tavistock Place,
what's the French film
I wanted to see?
Or perhaps I'll go to a gallery
to see Paul Klee or do nothing
but keep walking and
buy a bright yellow notebook
to maybe make myself happy,
momentarily, or perhaps
I will, I will, I will... just be
free of commitments, thoughts
of running away
to do what? Take a leap...
go to Barbados, to Greece!
But I'm here and the sky is blue
some part of me says
there's so much to do,
hello? hello, it's me, again
summer's turning back to spring
the birds all jump up and sing!
I want to love myself again,

so I skip across the street,
London, London is the place for me.
I keep happy thoughts
to a tourist's beat;
barefoot Beatles crossing the road,
and didn't you see them?
But didn't hear a sound,
collapsed hysterical amongst all
the other screaming bodies,
they called you George, the quiet one,
amongst the others,
in a dormitory, four hundred miles
from home, nobody to come calling,
still a child all alone,
your mother and father
at the ski resort down the road...
a life spent
searching for a way back home.
Keep on the pavement,
avoid the cracks,
the sun is waxing and waning
between buildings, scaffolds.
Noon waiting on the horizon,
its black wings outstretched
filling up with hollowness,
it's always one or the other
with a brain like this, who needs enemies?
Now a thick cloud covers the sun.
How to manage? Rationalise,
hold fast. It will turn... that much we know,
but feel the

black wings outstretched,
the talons sinking in,
so now, and now, and now
I'm back again, in
that dark room...
warm, machines blinking,
nurses huddled out of earshot.
Like cabin crew
in a stalling flight, I watched faces
for panic in that room,
that dark terminal, full of endings,
watching the translucent tube exhume
green bags of bile.
"You realise how ill she is,"
one nurse said to me,
I nodded but didn't really, but then knew
an end had come, a quiet rupture
your eyes closed, white face,
hands smaller but thicker
than I recalled as I held one,
your hand I held, hand...
hand-written note on the bedside next day,
a shopping list of apples,
chicken, mashed potatoes.
"Call Tom?"
No more, I confess a strange
relief, even though too soon
to know the ending,
no more fears
or pained expectations,
no more normalised despair,

as my therapist says,
you are the wound
from which all wounds bleed,
a tributary
that runs unseen
that ties me to you,
and you to me...
and now my son-
yes, I have a son now too!
change your mood,
distract yourself;
count all the green things you can
see, one, two, three,
a little green man walking
and the bright spring trees,
now a woman in a green dress,
hair blown by the breeze.
How despairing, you must have been,
so bad you confessed leaving
all three of us on the road side,
threw yourself on the bonnet
of the car begging not be left,
until they put you away,
in a white room,
in a white building with green lawns,
the hospital Lucia Joyce
died in the year you arrived,
King Lear scenes,
electroshock despair,
sweated draconian remedies
to seek a cause...

but you were just lonely
and at war,
another child victim of the Anglo norm,
the bloated coronation of expectation,
the corroded artefacts of golden
regimes,
unspoken shame
and isolation,
a product of the lie
that children are resilient
to pain, they bounce, you know,
instead, the truth, they mould
then harden like clay,
until we are dropped having
to piece ourselves together
again and again.
Open the aperture, soften the focus,
feel your hands warm in the sun,
the air on your arms,
keep to the sunny side of the street,
these are the techniques.
You're no different, look at you
passing in the mirrored glass;
swimming languid
on the summer street, a free man
with his sleeves rolled
breathing in the city heat.
Along Tavistock Place past
Gino's barber,
The Marquis Cornwallis,
the Chinese acupuncture,

the Italian cafe and
happy folk drinking frappé,
the bright fruit stand,
with oranges, lemons and limes.
Yes, we're living and you're gone,
gone with your pink reading glasses,
and beige pastel pink
wellington boots.
Gone with your bedside post-it notes,
your powder blue hairbrush,
gone in your everyday
black clothes, your morning espresso
with one sweetener,
with your banana mashed
on white toast.
Gone with your body you never
made peace with; its chronic inflammation,
your irritable bowels
and endless prescriptions,
Naproxen, Ibuprofen, Benzedrine, Amitriptyline,
gone with black coffee and Clozapine,
gone with Prozac,
white wine,
gone with your body and your mind,
gone with black and white thinking,
gone with life and death,
gone with scorched earth realities,
gone with mountains of delusions,
of driving around after dark
looking for bodies in the road,
blue lights of your causing,

looking for blood splats on door handles.
gone with death,
gone with love,
gone all-encompassing, smothering life,
gone with late-night calls
of care and despair,
gone with the fabric of all things,
gone with nature, gone with nurture,
gone with truth to leave
a world behind and awakening
empty-hearted and helpless,
gone with voice and face,
each day going, a pyre in the darkness
fading, your face expression
no longer visible, stop.
Where am I? Past the Horse Hospital,
the open door of the Friend At Hand;
dark stooped silhouettes,
the comforting stench
of polish on beer soured floors.
Ah… a long hesitation.
but the bright day waits;
I turn towards Russell Square
happy, blinking in the sun,
beneath the green, breathing trees,
international students, and
au pairs with prams,
toddlers running half naked
through the fountains.
I loosen my thoughts, I look above
which window was T.S. Eliot's ?

I think of Bloomsbury and bright red buses
and maybe I will take one,
or maybe I'll keep walking
as I am, as morning turns to noon,
not losing hope, catching my face
in mirrored glass,
no less happy, no less sad,
just another still alive
and walking through the world
that you made.

Tom Harding – Biography

Tom Harding lives in Northampton, UK with his wife and son. He is a poet and illustrator. He keeps a website of his work at www.tomharding.net. He is also the editor of the Northampton Poetry Review. His debut collection of poetry, NIGHT WORK, and its follow up, AFTERNOON MUSIC, were released by Palewell Press in 2017 and 2020 respectively.

Palewell Press

Palewell Press is an independent publisher handling poetry, fiction and non-fiction with a focus on human rights, social history, and the environment. The Editor may be reached via enquiries@palewellpress.co.uk